Sacred Messages from Sacred Ireland

Sacred Messages from Sacred Ireland

Jane Donald

Halleluaj Press

First published in 2010 by
Halleluaj Press
Kilbride
Co. Carlow
Ireland

Photographs: Jane Donald

ISBN: 978-0-9566615-0-0

Book design and layout: Niamh Power, Print Design Services, Ireland

Cover design: Niamh Power and Jane Donald

Printed by: Gráficas Castuera.

Contents

Preface

This book is a celebration of the lifeforce that runs through all living things. It is made up of messages brought to me through nature and received from Sacred Sites in Ireland. Simply put, I act as a sort of interpreter of the vibration I feel from the trees, lakes, rivers, mountains and Sacred Sites I visit. *Sacred Messages from Sacred Ireland* came about as a result of my search for self-empowerment and healing. It is one of the positive outcomes of a ten-year struggle to regain my health and well-being and to recover from Myalgic Encephalomyelitis, a condition known as Post-Viral Chronic Fatigue Syndrome and Immune Dysfunction in North America.

As the birth of this book and the path I have been following since I first became ill are so intricately linked, I would like to share my experience with you. It has been a difficult, but ultimately enlightening and life-changing journey.

The first time I was conscious of my body being under any physical strain was back in May 1999 when I was just twenty five. While water skiing, I pulled the hamstring in my left leg very badly. This injury triggered a devastating spiral into severe ill health which was to last until 2009. ME changed the direction, understanding and outlook I had on life beyond anything I could have imagined. Despite continual visits to a physiotherapist, the muscle in my leg wasted. At the time I was very actively involved in playing senior club hockey in Dublin. I was struggling to stay fit and keep up and subsequently trained harder and harder.

That lasted until one evening in October 2000 when I felt a blockage and pain in the area below the centre of my ribcage (which I now know to be the solar plexus chakra) and I could not get my arms and legs to work. The following day in work I felt ill, lacking in energy and nauseous, so I left and went to see my doctor. I got an appointment to see a gastric consultant for February 2001. In the intervening four months I trundled on with a sick stomach, blinding headaches, lack of energy, fatigue and a feeling that I can only describe as being a nasty cross between flu, food poisoning and a hangover.

When I finally saw the consultant in question I was diagnosed as suffering from chronic fatigue syndrome. Since there is no established medical treatment, the advice I was given was 'to rest, not to climb any mountains,' (I like hill walking) and 'to continue working'. There was no mention of a serious neurological illness or the term Myalgic Encephalomyelitis.

In my complete ignorance I decided to take a break. However, being the lover of sports that I am, I chose a snow ski holiday reasoning, quite seriously, it was all downhill! This proved to be a big mistake, my body could not take the stress of the physical exercise and it made the illness very severe for the next eight years. Physical exercise even just walking would be an impossibility for me for almost a decade.

The general medical consensus is that if you have ME for longer than two years, there is little chance of a recovery. Myalgic means muscle pain and encephalomyelitis means an inflammation of the spinal cord. Varying degrees of disability, illness and disruption are caused to people's lives by the symptoms. It is a complex and debilitating physiological illness involving neurological and endocrinal dysfunction and immune system dysregulation which is not improved by bed rest and can worsen with physical or mental exertion. It is estimated there are at least 12,000 ME sufferers in Ireland and 17 million worldwide.

In May of 2000 I found a doctor who had some experience in trying to treat ME and energy problems. Prior to this the only medical test I could get was an adrenal saliva test, which a doctor I contacted in the USA did for me by post. Such is the difficulty in getting appropriate medical treatment in Ireland. Pacing yourself and resting are very important in the attempt to stave off the worst symptoms. There are few doctors in Ireland or worldwide with even a basic understanding of ME or a willingness to learn more about it. The fact is that many doctors remain uneducated about ME and there is, as yet, no medical diagnostic test or agreed established course of medical treatment. Each patient experiences ME differently and can have a wide variety of seemingly non-related symptoms.

In August 2000 my twin sister Lyn who had been collecting magazines about holistic therapies told me that she had read that Reiki might be useful for ME sufferers. I had never heard of Reiki and was sceptical as I knew nothing at all about it. The next day I was in a shop when I saw a huge poster advertising Reiki sessions. I made an appointment immediately. It had an amazing effect, like plugging in to a power source and getting recharged.

I began to learn Reiki myself, completing the three levels to become a Reiki Master. The meditation involved proved very useful as I was experiencing a lot of sleep disturbance, ranging from insomnia and sleep deprivation to sleeping for seventeen hour stretches at a time. It helped me calm down the "tired but wired" feeling in my body, a trademark of ME. As I was forced to spend long periods resting and lying down over the following eight years I had ample occasion to improve my meditation techniques.

The main turning point came five years into the ME when I got stuck on the bathroom floor for four days without being able to reach my mobile phone. I had been having difficulty standing up and often could not feel my body from the waist down. Later I was to find out that I had a lack of oxygen going to my brain. Physical collapses were part of my daily life, as I was pushing myself to remain in employment, but usually I was able to reach a chair or bed and I always kept my mobile close at hand.

It was during these physical collapses that I found meditation particularly useful to remain calm, patient and emotionally adjusted. This incident happened after a particularly stressful and busy publishing deadline in work. On another occasion I had got stuck while out walking the dog on a damp autumn day. I had no other choice but to lie in the field for six hours before I managed to crawl on my hands and knees back to the house and warmth. My dog Oscar was very good about it, waiting patiently by my side throughout. Oscar was a wonderful source of strength, always happy to see me no matter what state I was in.

At some stage during the four days on the bathroom floor I swore in utter frustration and desperation, 'Jesus Christ give me a break!' A curious thing happened, I felt like I was floating above and outside of my body. It felt like a wonderful freedom, no illness, suffering or fear just a sense of being still and that was really me. I was not just the body that I could see lying on the floor beneath me. I was something more.

When I recovered, I wondered what I could do to improve the situation in terms of how my work was organized. I telephoned my Mum to explain where I had been, she was concerned and worried obviously but had no idea what advice to give me. She felt, as I did, that I needed to keep my job going for practical purposes. At the office, I knew that if certain work procedures and practices were tweaked, it would be an enormous relief to me, but that solution proved not to be possible. I went to my local health centre to see if I could get help there. The nurse actually laughed in my face and told me I had an illness 'from the twilight zone' and kept asking me how much I was earning and pointing out how young I was and how well I looked.

The difficulty with ME is that it is not recognised or known about by the medical establishment. It is not part of the health system so any treatment, medical or holistic, you try in an effort to improve your situation, must be paid for and so you obviously need an income. In practical terms ME creates the following dilemma for many patients: Is it better to stop work in order to rest but have no money or should one struggle on working and be able to afford treatments but not get enough rest for them to be fully effective?

I was in a situation where my employers wanted me to stay on in my job and I could work from home. I decided to continue working and made a substantial investment in various treatments to try to heal myself. I really believed I could. I had had a strong feeling from the very beginning of my illness (despite all evidence to the contrary, what doctors had told me and what I had read about this "incurable" disease) that I would get better and that I was supposed to be learning something from the whole experience.

Coming up against a brick wall as regards human help and solutions I pondered what else to do. I tried to remember and figure out how I had managed to achieve that state of stillness on the bathroom floor where I had experienced wellness for the first time in five years. I realised that when swearing in frustration and despair that I had inadvertently really asked for a break and that is exactly what I was given. Up to this point I had been reading, researching and focusing on medical and holistic ways of relieving physical symptoms. But armed with this new experience I began to focus more on my ultimate goal, what I really needed, how I wanted my life to be. I simply asked to be shown how to be well and happy.

A curious thing began to unfold. I started to get led to people and treatments that could help me at a given moment in time, the right time. I found myself on the Internet site of a Welsh lady who had recovered from ME. I had already tried and implemented most of the advice she was giving but my interest was grabbed by a programme called the Empower Programme I looked at the website, it promised to help me "connect to my higher intelligence" to "unlock my potential within". I still did not understand what was involved or what this meant so I gave the woman in Wales a call to find out more. 'It sounds wacky,' she said 'but it works, there is even a section specifically for ME.' Based on my conversation with her I ordered the programme.

It turned out to be a remarkable, in fact dramatic programme. I could literally 'command' my own body and mind to make positive changes instantaneously, purely by asking. This led to spontaneous physical movements where the physical body went into a state of vibration as a result of the "Higher Self" implementing these instructions. My body literally moved of its own accord and went into vibration while I was doing the programme. It was very strange, but it was helping greatly.

Gradually I found I was making it my own, incorporating it constantly into my daily life as the healing brought more and more issues to my conscious mind for healing. I asked more and more for healing, awareness, insights and anything that would make me well and happy. I started to use the meditation skills I had learnt to visualise myself happy and healthy. You often hear the phrase "listen to your body" but I also started to talk to my body constantly, to ask my body to regenerate itself and to ask my physical organs, body systems, cells, electrons, protons etc to work properly and to their optimum for me and my body to heal itself.

After five years the doctor I had been attending decided to test me for mercury poisoning. I had no amalgam fillings in my teeth and so it had not been considered a problem. It is rare to find a doctor in Ireland who would even think to test for mercury or heavy metal poisoning. Mercury can come from a number of possible sources including amalgam fillings, vaccinations, fish, crop seeds and sprays. Mercury can be transferred from the mother to a foetus in the womb. Heavy metal poisoning is also implicated in several other neurological illnesses for example Parkinson's and Alzeimhers. It turned out I had ten times what is considered the safe level of mercury in my body. It took three tough years to get the mercury out of my body using mercury chelation, infrared saunas, chlorea, charcoal, the Empower program and TBM (Total Body Modification).

Shortly after the mercury-poisoning discovery a holistic therapist I had been attending recommended that I see a therapist called Roy Stapleton who practices TBM. I followed the advice as it felt positive. TBM involves muscle testing to find areas of the body that are weak and it then corrects the Functional Physiology (how the body works). On the first visit Roy identified and switched off three viruses. it felt great, like my body was no longer fighting a huge battle against some unknown enemy. I attended Roy for a year for regular sessions before he suggested that I learn TBM. He was teaching it and thought I would be good at it. I was still very much struggling to function and hold down the remnants of a "normal" life but again it felt correct for me at that moment so I did it.

TBM is a channelled healing technique from Utah in the USA. When learning TBM, I found I was being overwhelmed by the energy and was finding even the effort of sitting upright difficult, let alone reading or understanding the manual. Roy began to adjust and do the corrections on me. Once he did that, I was able to repeat them spontaneously. I was learning by transference. Now I practised TBM on myself on a daily basis. It was like I had known this information all my life but had somehow forgotten it. The only thing I can compare it to is the natural instinct I had while playing sport, innately knowing what to do and when to do it. It was obvious to me.

When I was qualified and wanted to start taking on TBM clients, I consciously put the thought out there; how do I go about getting clients? I received an email from the ME Trust asking me to do a piece for the *Irish Independent Health Supplement* on useful treatments for ME. There was a photo of me on the front page and inside was an article on TBM. The phone began to ring with people looking for appointments. As I practised TBM, I found I was healing myself and helping others. People also started to ring and ask me to clear their house of negative energy. Doing healing sessions on people or house clearing was not a type of work that I ever had any notion of doing. I had learnt the TBM to treat myself and improve my own health situation but now it was leading me down another path.

While receiving a TBM treatment from Roy one day, I was lying on the plinth relaxing with my eyes closed when I felt a profound shift in my energy and feeling of well-being. I opened my eyes to see Roy pale and shaking, clutching the corner of his desk. 'Jesus Christ' I said, 'Are you ok?' Roy replied, 'That is the point. Jesus Christ just came down and poured your mercury load into a chalice. I saw him.' So it was working! If I asked and followed the energy I was being led where I needed to go.

In November 2006, a colleague sent me an email about a treatment called the Perrin Technique and how an osteopath in Manchester called Dr Raymond Perrin had "accidentally cured" an ME patient while treating them for back problems. Dr Perrin wrote a book and trademarked his treatment calling it the Perrin Technique. I made an appointment for December 2006 and flew to Manchester to see him with my twin Lyn. You need a chaperone as part of the treatment involves the osteopath massaging the lymphatic system in the chest to relieve the toxic load on the body.

Lyn had been experiencing similar health problems to me since she had a bad car accident. She had been diagnosed with fibromyalgia but I figured she also had ME, as anecdotally it is hereditary. I thought Dr Perrin would be interested in identical twins for his own research and education in treating people with ME. He also diagnosed Lyn with ME and told me that I had so little oxygen going to my brain I should not be standing up and walking around let alone working. My head was 'like a deflated football,' he explained.

We began flying to Manchester every fortnight until March 2007 when an osteopath in Dublin started to do the Perrin Technique. Part of the Perrin Technique includes a self-treatment regime with self-massage and back rotation exercises. But Lyn and I both found when we combined it with the Empower Programme and said 'give me what I need to have the best Perrin technique healing for me for my highest good,' our bodies moved spontaneously correcting themselves energetically. Again we had learnt by transference healing.

I found the Perrin Technique to be a very difficult treatment for someone who is ill and weakened with ME. Even though I had already done two years of mercury detoxing before I even started the Perrin Technique. You actually need to be quite physically robust and well as it is very tough going and quite dramatic when you first start and the toxins that have built up in your body for years begin to shift. You definitely get worse before you get better.

Browsing in a book shop one day around St Patrick's Day 2008, my husband, Paul, came over to me and said, 'there are CDs over there you need to look at.' It was still a novelty to be back out in shops since years of ME had meant avoiding them. I still tired easily so I simply said to myself, 'show me which CDs I need for my highest good.'

I was drawn to two CDs by best selling authors, Esther and Gerry Hicks entitled *The Amazing Power of Deliberate Intent – Living the Art of Allowing*. I started listening to these CDs knowing nothing about *The Teachings of Abraham* which Esther Hicks channels. They had a profound effect on me, with symptoms of ME that had been going on for eight years just dissolving. Again it was like I had known this information all my life but had somehow forgotten it. So I listened to every bit of *The Teachings of Abraham*. I learnt for the first time about *The Law of Attraction* in a book called *"Ask and It Is Given."* I realised I had been consciously using the *Law of Attraction* without knowing what to call it since I had stumbled on the realisation after the bathroom floor fiasco.

Shortly after this in April 2008 I attended a talk given by Dr Deepak Chopra. Again I had the same sensation that I had known this information all my life but had somehow forgotten it. His advice is to ask the big questions in life. I consciously put the thought out there: "What is my life purpose?"

Four days later at a World TBM Conference in France, a curious thing happened. A TBM practitioner from Las Vegas began talking to me about my throat chakra being blocked and said, 'You are trying to make a change.' 'I know,' I said, 'I am trying to give up work.' 'Ah' he said, 'what you need to know is your life purpose'. 'Yes.' I replied in shock. 'It is not this, not TBM' he said. 'I think it has to do with publishing. I work in publishing.' I replied. 'Ah' he said again. 'Have you heard of Esther and Gerry Hicks?' I nodded. 'You are going to channel books.' I was stunned and disbelieving. I had been given the answer to the question I had asked only four days earlier.

I came home wondering what this could possibly be all about and how would I ever know how to channel books! I had been reading *The Artist's Way* by Julia Cameron. There is an exercise where you write three pages of meditation she calls *"Morning Pages"*. I am not a morning person and so I was trying to do it in the evening. I was struggling with the whole thing, nothing much was happening, no flow; it felt like I was forcing it.

One evening, spontaneously like automatic writing, my hand took off answering questions I had just been wondering about earlier in my head. I was writing furiously, not knowing what I had written until I read it back. It contained amazing, really profound advice on all the questions that I had been asking in my head. I followed the advice and continued to ask questions and get answers about how to improve my physical, mental and emotional well-being. I began to wonder again about channelling books. How would anyone be able to do that and how would one go about doing it?

During the summer of 2008, I was wandering from my office building to the canteen when I felt drawn to a big old sycamore tree in the middle of a roundabout in the business park. I could feel a sense of buzzing or vibration around my head. The next tree did the same and on the way back a beech tree did the same. When I got back to my desk, I took out a piece of paper and wrote down the message each tree had given me. It was like a stream of consciousness or automatic writing.

For the next eighteen months I continued to follow the energy and inspiration where I was drawn to it, and to write and collect messages. Sometimes I would just be driving along and be drawn to a particular place.

Other days I would set out with friends and just go where we felt inspired and drawn to, always following intuition and where the energy was taking us. "Mystery tours" we call them! My instinct was to take photos and collect messages for this book. When I asked what to call the book.... my hand wrote *Sacred Messages from Sacred Ireland*.

When I asked how to publish the book, my hand wrote... set up a publishing company and call it Halleluaj Press. Since I had started to feel better I had been in the habit of shouting "Halleluaj!" as I got out of bed because I was so happy to be feeling better and I was finding standing upright and functioning was becoming so much easier!

The messages are presented exactly as I received them. The punctuation and the spelling were given to me. Hence the spelling of the word Halleluaj. The energy was insistent on the spelling of Halleluaj. The messages are grouped according to county only to help the reader to locate the places in their minds eye easily. Remember this book is the story of my healing journey so it reflects places and counties that I was able to visit as I carried on living my everyday life with its ups and downs, and responsibilities.

The messages were received and the photos taken in the moment. Considerations like the weather, the time of year, the season or the best conditions for photography were secondary. The important thing was the inspiration and the magic of the moment in that place where I was inspired to be at that exact moment of time for me. This book is about living and being in the moment. It is about being vibrationally aligned to your source energy in that moment.

Each message was received upon visiting the place, feeling the energy and being in the vibration. So the message and the photographs are integral to each other. The messages in this book are meant for feeling, quieten your mind and allow yourself to feel the vibration of the messages. Feel them in your heart, the heart knows and is an ancient wisdom. They are lessons and nourishment for the soul. The mind and ego give us a contrast to the heart and soul.

In August 2008, I was doing a healing session on a lady called Carmel Costello. At one point she asked me what I was doing. Since I was following my guidance and intuitively healing, I asked myself, 'What am I doing?' The answer came back, 'Working with the angels.' This was news to me, but because I trusted the guidance, I answered 'Working with the angels,' and Carmel said no more. After the healing session, she asked whether I knew I was doing IET. 'What is IET?' I answered, never having heard of it before.

IET (Integrated Energy Therapy) is a channelled healing technique by Steven Thayer in the USA that uses Archangel Ariel's energy. Carmel is a practitioner and Master Teacher. Subsequently I did the course and became a qualified IET practitioner. This was the first time I learnt or read anything about angels in my life. The only prior knowledge I had about angels was from the Christmas story. I had overheard people talking about angels when I was learning Reiki years earlier but had not paid much attention.

As I had been regaining my physical health, pregnancy seemed like a real possibility. I was now thirty five years old and had been struggling with my health since the age of twenty five. My doctor had decided to send me to a fertility consultant. I had the appointment date. Given the ignorance and prejudice surrounding ME in Ireland he was protecting me and warning that the particular consultant he was sending me to did not believe in ME. Therefore I was not to mention ME or mercury poisoning, I was just to say I had been "a bit tired." The consultant would be unhappy that I had been on steroids for eight years but she was the best in her field.

The anecdotal record of the treatment of ME patients by the medical system is not a proud one and I have had personal experience of the negativity. As ME is a holistic illness in that it affects every system in the body, it is not an illness suited to a mechanistic type medical system or model of specialisation where each doctor only knows about one area of the body and not about the whole. I was not happy; I did not have much faith or trust in a doctor who was so blinkered. My feeling was that I would be fine and get pregnant when my body was ready. So I asked for guidance and gave thanks for a baby at the best time for me. The conventional wisdom would be not to get your hopes up. I did the opposite. I believed and expected to have a happy healthy pregnancy and baby using the healing methods I had learnt.

A healer from Cork, John Collins was recommended to me in September 2008. I followed the positive vibe I felt and went to see him. I instantly felt a deep connection of mutual understanding. He has a powerful energy. He read me like an open book. He was the first person I met who knew how to help me manage and use my sensitivity to energy. How to consciously switch it on and off and also how to tune in and tune out of energy. He explained how to protect my own energy levels and well-being and how to only use my sensitivity to energy when I need to, for example to tune in to a person or situation.

He also explained that I was Green Man energy like him. This explained the deep feeling of connection to nature and why nature was giving me messages. It also explained my ten years working in a gardening magazine and my love of nature. Regarding the baby, he told me I was correct. I did not need medical intervention, I was simply to keep giving thanks for the baby I expected to come. After ninety minutes of talking to this man, I realised I felt like myself in my physical body and knew who I was for the first time since I was a very young child. My well-being improved so dramatically after just one visit to John Collins, I stopped taking the sixty supplements a day and weaned myself off the prescription drugs that my doctor had me taking since 2001.

For some time when I asked questions about my job, the message was to give it up at Christmas 2008. I had been experiencing resistance to this message mainly due to financial concerns but now they dissolved and I handed in my notice in work intending to do TBM healing for a living and follow the energy to where it took me and collect these messages. It felt wonderful. In hindsight the timing was perfect given the economic downturn globally in 2009, which affected all businesses and jobs greatly.

2009 proved to be an emotional roller coaster of a year. In January I had a positive pregnancy test. When I did a scan it showed that I was already twenty weeks pregnant. The next day my dog Oscar died. The day after my second scan in March, my Dad died. He had been suffering from bone cancer. He died following a failed operation to relieve bleeding in his brain, the result of a fall. Thankfully in the end he died peacefully in his sleep twenty minutes after I had done healing on him. My Mum and I were with him.

It had not been possible to tell from the scan whether our baby was a boy or girl. When I asked what the name of our child was, my hand wrote Samuel, Jacob. We had not for a moment thought of either of these names. I looked up Samuel in the baby name book; it is a biblical name meaning "gift asked of God." Samuel, Jacob was born on 30th June 2009 to much joy.

For most of July my Mum had been in hospital having tests. She had had a liver transplant in December 2003 following primary liver cancer. The cancer was caused by dye put into her body prior to an operation as a young child. Now, again, in August she was diagnosed with cancer, and unfortunately it had spread extensively. She died less than seven weeks later, roughly six months after Dad. One day just before my Mum died, she woke and said to my brother and I, 'What are we all doing here anyway, what is it all about?' I remember thinking she is not much longer for this world if she has started to ask questions like that. My mother also died peacefully in her sleep shortly after Lyn had done healing on her.

The messages in this book often reflect questions I have been asking myself about life and death over the last eighteen months. Remember energy always follows intention. This is the sharing of a personal experience over several years for what it is worth. What have I learnt? Open your heart and mind. Allow yourself to awaken to a higher consciousness. Ask for help and guidance and then when you sense a response, follow the energy when and where it leads you and take appropriate action. Trust your feelings and intuition. Do what feels good, not what you think you should do. Always act from your heart with pure intention and you will have inner happiness and well being.

Your body has the power to heal itself if you can learn to find and tap into that power and allow that power. I now have made a habit of self-healing and meditation on a daily basis, just like brushing my teeth. I am still, and always will be, filled with questions about life. Life still has ups and downs, dramas and challenges but I know now how to tap into the energy of inner peace, stillness, knowing and wisdom that runs through us all. Don't expect it to be easy, but be easy with yourself and those around you and enjoy life. I trust this book will be of genuine help, empowerment and enjoyment to people in their everyday life.

Love and best wishes,

Jane Donald

Jane Donald
www.janedonaldloveandlight.com

Useful websites
Empower Programme www.empower-disc.co.uk
TBM (Total Body Modification) www.tbmireland.ie
Perrin Technique www.theperrinclinic.com
Integrated Energy Therapy www.integratedenergytherapy.com
Irish ME Trust www.imet.ie
CFS/ME Support Group www.irishmecfs.org
Esther and Gerry Hicks (*Teachings of Abraham and The Law of Attraction*) www.abraham-hicks.com

As with all Holistic Healing and Therapies, nothing in this book should be construed as a claim to "cure" any particular condition. Healing is not intended to replace medical treatment and should be viewed as complementary to it. A professional healer will not "diagnose" or tell you to discontinue medical treatment.

Acknowledgements

Thanks and love to Paul Huggard, Samuel Donald-Huggard and Lyn Donald for everything as always. Special thanks to Carmel Costello, Anne Whelan, Emer McHale, Asta Kelly, Eithne Kennedy and Olive Dermody for coming on wonderful, magical, mystery tours with me to create this book. A million thank yous to John Collins for his wonderful healing gift and his pure intention using it. Thank you to Roy Stapleton for all the TBM sessions and guidance in unlocking my potential. Thanks to Mary Cummins and Asta Kelly for editing work and guidance. Thanks to Helen Dunne and Gerry Daly for publishing advice. Thanks to Richie Kavanagh for the use of the photograph of my parents. Thanks to the landowners. Finally thanks to Niamh Power for design and production. Extra special thanks to all who were kind, gentle and patient with me while I was ill, it was a wonderful, much appreciated gift to receive.

Love and best wishes Jane Donald

Emer McHale and Eithne Kennedy

Carmel Costello

Lyn Donald and Olive Dermody

Anne Whelan and Samuel Donald-Huggard

Paul Huggard

Asta Kelly and Samuel Donald-Huggard

In loving memory and appreciation of my parents

Stuart and Linda who passed over in 2009.

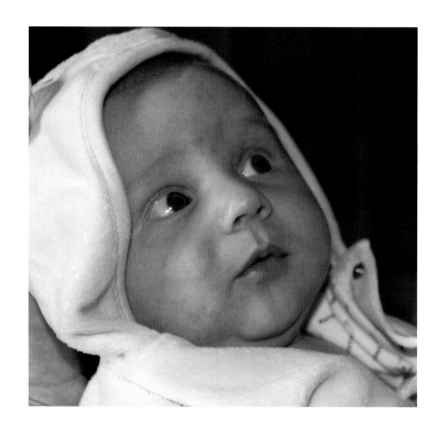

Message from Samuel

Love one another,
Love yourself,
Love every bit of yourself
Your body, thoughts, emotions,
let yourself be love,
let love be you,
now and always,
This is the lesson.
Thank you God.

Introduction

These Sacred Messages are channelled through Jane Donald to be given to people who are ready to receive them. They are blessings for mankind and lessons for life. They allow people to connect to their inner power and appreciate their own lifeforce that courses through their physical bodies and which unites them with every other living consciousness in the Universe. It is for people to understand that the Universe is vibrational and all they are and the world is, is energy, love and light, a mirage of light, a combination of atoms, electrons and protons that gives us the image of reality that we see as our environment, our earth. It is for people to understand that the earth is part of a greater cosmos of planets, stars, moon and sun. It is part of eternity, part of timelessness that is difficult for mankind to understand, but fundamental to mankind to make the leap in their understanding and connection to the lifeforce known as God and every other word mankind has ever used for God or the power of the Universe.

Ballymoon Castle, near Bagenalstown

It is for mankind to realise the importance of their dreams, to realise the importance of their thoughts, as vibrational messages asking and requesting from the Universe, to manifest and to be created in their lives. Learn to consciously create, wake up and know that you are the creator and arcitects of your own life, it is not just happening to you. You are creating it whether you know you are or not on some level.

1

Mount Leinster and Blackstairs Mountains

Halleluaj, praise be to the mighty one for all the splendour of today and all the splendour in front of your eyes, around your ears, for you to smell, taste and know. It is for all to appreciate, once awareness is allowed and once consciousness is given to the mighty Mother Nature and her wonders.

River Burren at its source in the
Blackstairs Mountains

Allow yourself time to contemplate, time to reflect, time to
be, flow with the stream, downhill, around obstacles, let
your life flow from your source as the river does always
downstream, always downhill with the wind behind your
back. Life is for flowing. It is not meant to be a battle.
Focus on what you want and life will always be downhill,
downstream for you and joyous living is yours.

The Nine Stones, Blackstairs Mountains

Allow your strength to be your ease of mind, allow your strength to be your
ease of heart, allow your strength to be your ease to show compassion,
kindness and love to all living things, as you want to be, allow them to be.
Allow all living things to thrive, to fit in harmony as the creator has designed,
allow all living things the freedom to be and to be recognised as they are and
as they want to be.

Back Lawn,
Raheenwood,
Fenagh

Allow, allow, allow the natural world to be as it was created, not exploited for gain but lived with and for, in harmony with all living beings and mankind. The earth provides plenty without need for abuse, without need for exploitation — work with Mother Earth not against her — allow yourself to be part of Mother Earth, feel her power, her presence, her love and desire to provide you with plenty and then allow your heart to open, to protect and preserve her dignity, allow her love and her kindness.

Nine Acres, Raheenwood, Fenagh

Allow all to be, all to flourish, all to feel their hearts, all to follow their faith. Allow all to become their dream, allow all to become their wish, their want of potential and life, to be one with all that is the lifeforce that flows through all living things. Allow yourself to allow others to be this lifeforce, to live fully connected to their source. Energy in perfect vibrational harmony.

Raheenwood, Fenagh

It is for mankind to know the love of Mother Earth for all living things including them. It is for mankind to understand that Mother Earth is here to provide all you need but the ways of the natural world need to be respected and worked with rather than fought against, exploited and raped. It is for mankind to live and love in harmony with all living things, be they plant, mineral, animal, insect or bird. Allow respect for all living things and live joyously in their care and love, in harmony and peace forever.

Garden at Raheenwood, Fenagh

Thank you for the love and care of nature,
Thank you for the harmony with nature,
Thank you for the love and truth of all,
Thank you for allowing all to be.
Thank you, thank you, thank you.

Temple Moling Cemetery

Allow, allow, allow the splendour of nature to be your guide, follow the seasons, follow the crops of fruit, berries and grain and allow the animals to be part of your ecosystem. Allow all to play their part in the cycle of life — allow yourself to be part of the natural way of things, the natural rhythms of nature and the natural world — as you are part of it, it is part of you and all is as one as it should be and as it is — let it be, so it is — so it be.

St. Moling's Well, St. Mullins

Halleluaj celebrate each moment, each day,
in the moment, the time is now, the time to
be present is now. Awareness of the present
is the key to inner peace and happiness.

St. Mullins

It is for all mankind to know of and to love Christ, to know of and love the father/mother God, to know of and to love the kingdom of nature, the glory of mankind as part of nature.

Temple na Boe, St. Mullins

Allow all to live, allow all to be, allow all to have an
opportunity to fulfil their potential, it is for God to create
and mankind to allow.

Woods at Clashganny near Borris

Glory to all mankind, glory to all God's kingdom, glory to the flowers, glory to the trees, glory to the ferns, glory to the birds, glory to the river, glory to the animals, glory to the insects. Halleluaj, halleluaj.

River Barrow at Clashganny near Borris

Allow glory and greatness in your life, see the wonder in yourself, you are a miracle, you are a precious being, a precious spirit, a precious soul, you are part of the greater cosmos, without you the cosmos would be incomplete in this moment, ponder that and allow yourself be a part of that.

Ring of Rath, Hilltop Fort, Tullow

Allow all to see the beauty of your soul,
Allow all to see the beauty in your eyes,
Allow all to see the beauty in your smile,
Allow all to see the beauty in your thoughts,
Allow all to see the beauty in your speech,
In your actions — always know that
You are beautiful within — look within
And allow it come out and shine.

Oak Tree at Ring of Rath, Hilltop Fort, Tullow

It is for mankind to know wisdom is in their heart not their head, you can study and train all your life but it is useless if you do not live from your heart, from that ancient wisdom.

Hawthorn trees and pond at Ring of Rath, Hilltop Fort, Tullow

Allow all to be in nature, allow yourself to be in nature, you are nature, nature is you. Anything else is resistance to your true self.

Hawthorn Trees at Ring of Rath, Hilltop Fort, Tullow

Allow all to be one and one to be all. Allow all to be one and one to be one. Allow all to be one and one to be none. Allow all as it is, and as it is in this moment, in this moment all is well and as it should be, one and all.

Hawthorn Hedgerow, Kilbride

Celebrate the berry, celebrate the flowers, the leaf and the thorn. Anchor your roots deep in the soil, reach for the skies. Stand together, stand tall, in your environment. Stand and enjoy the breeze of life as it flies past your face — enjoy the breeze of life as it shows you the creator's presence in your hair and the coolness on your skin. Stand still and be aware that all is as it should be — that all is as it is and all is well — thank you.

The Moat, Castlegrace

Allow, allow, allow, it is the wonder of mankind that they cannot see
and understand energy, it is the power that powers all living things,
but all mankind can see is wealth, material goods and money as
power. Do you think on your death bed you are going to ask what
your bank balance is? Or are you going to be calling on God for help?
Wake up now in the present, moment to moment and see the real
power behind mankind and all life on earth. Thank you.

Cloch an Phoill (Aghade Holed Stone)

Allow yourself the greatness of being true to your soul,
true to your soul's purpose, journey with the purpose,
follow that journey, follow your soul, your soul is as
ancient as time, as wise as it is ancient, follow that
wisdom and you will have joy every moment of your life.

Weeping Ash Tree, Aghade

Halleluaj, praise be to nature in all its wonder, allow all that lives and breathes the love of your heart — allow all that lives the energy of your soul — it is your wonder — your true purpose in this life — allow your power to shine — wake up and let your light shine.

Hawthorn Trees, Aghade

Halleluaj — it for mankind to allow themselves to flourish by tapping into their inner power, their inner knowledge, their inner light. It is for mankind to know their own soul in order to evolve and become all they can be. Allow yourself to shine, to light up, to be a beacon to the world — embrace your own power — do not be afraid — you need to do this for yourself — for yourself alone.

Tulip Tree, Aghade

Allow yourself to feel beautiful, know the beauty of
your soul. Allow yourself all of your love, know the
love is always there for you, absolutely and
completely — thank you.

Garden at Aghade

Look to nature, look to the ecosystems, look to your part in that life giving, you are part of that not separate from it, or above it, or in charge of it. It is part of you and you are part of it, as one now and forever, and always as eternity.

River Slaney at Aghade Bridge

It is not for us to know all, it is enough for us to be and to know that we are, we need only to acknowledge and give thanks for all the greatness in a moment. You, the water, the trees, the dogs, the grass, we are all connected as one as the energy of life flows through us and in us. You do not need more or less, that is all there is and all there ever will be. Centre yourself in your soul and away from your mind and live in that state. All else is an illusion, a mirage, a trick of the light.

Pine Trees near Aghade Bridge

It is in the soul of mankind lie the answers, lie the knowledge
that unlocks the mystery, allow yourself to connect to your soul
on a daily basis through quiet contemplation and inward
momentum to your very soul.
Allow beauty in all that you see, allow faith in all that you see,
allow courage in all that you see — love all that you see.

Beech Trees near Aghade Bridge

Allow all to be and to worship, allow all to be as they are or as they believe themselves to be. Allow all to follow their beliefs as they see fit, allow all to be and behave as their inner beings allows and guides them to.

You are a magnificent soul, a magnificent wonderful being of light — shine your light, bring people to you for love, show them love and compassion — thank you always, love always.

Beech Trees near Aghade Bridge

Say it loud this world is wonderful and graceful, wonderful and
true, it is what I make of it, it is what I want it to be, It is as I
see it, hear it, feel it, live it. Wake now and feel the wonder, see
the wonder, hear the wonder, wake now.
Allow yourself, allow each other, allow all beings the love, the
care, the respect you want in your life — thank you.

River Douglas at Aghade

Allow all to rest in your being, allow all to relax in your
knowing, allow all to be and just be and just be, it is alright to
concentrate on being rather than doing. Being creates more than
doing if you realise how to utilise the power within — the
vibration of love, peace and harmony. Thank you.

Hawthorn Hedge on Banks of River Douglas, Aghade

It is fun to be alive, wake up now and live, stop your idle slumber of day to day habits and routines, allow the magic, allow the fun, allow the living of life in all its splendour and magnificence.

Aghade Church

Celebrate in love and
care in love and peace,
in love and harmony.
Look to nature — peace
and harmony, one and
only one, every being
part of an ecosystem,
every being dependant
and interlinked with
another. What makes
mankind assume any
different? Ignorance
and greed.

Beech Tree Lined avenue at Altamont Gardens

It is splendour to allow nature, to work with nature in creating splendour. Allow yourself the magic of nature, be a part of the magic of nature and all will be well. Mother Earth is generous to a fault but if it comes down to it Mother Nature knows tough love for your higher good.

Altamont Gardens

Allow all to know and love their God, their life giver, their lifeforce.
Allow all to know and love themselves.
Allow all to be as they are.
Allow all to be great in themselves and in their soul.

Allow all to be in their heart.
Allow all to shine from their heart.
Allow all to shine from their love.
Thank you God.

Deodar Cedar at Altamont Gardens

Wisdom is there if you ask, with free will, you need to ask
if you want help — know this and ask — it is an infinite
intelligence there for your use, there for you to use, ask
and it is given. Thank you God.

Ballykealey, Ballon

Allow yourself to be immersed in the lifeforce energy,
allow yourself to feel the lifeforce energy, ask to feel it,
ask to be guided by it every moment of your life, you are
blessed and welcome to all you want if you ask, it is
given. Ask and feel your lifeforce to fulfil your potential
and learn to love yourself and all the ones of
consciousness that you are, a blessed part of.

Deodar Cedar at Ballykealey

Allow greatness, allow love, allow your light to shine on all, not just your family but also your enemy, spread your powerful light on all, give kindness, give empathy, give love — allow your true goodness to flow out into the world around you, lead by example, lead by love. Thank you.

Atlantic Cedar at Ballykealey

It is for mankind to know that all is love, family is love, friends are love, enemies are love, see your world this way and allow love to dictate your behaviour and you will prosper and be blessed. Thank you.

Near Parkbridge

Celebrate the view, celebrate the greenness,
the bounty of nature and the healing of
nature, the pleasure of nature, the stillness
and greatness, the power and the splendour.
Celebrate, celebrate every day, all day,
thank you.

Deodar Cedar near Parkbridge

It is for all to know themselves, to know what they are truly capable of, look to the Masters, this potential can be yours also if you truly wish and follow your soul's instructions. Thank you.

Hills near Clonegal

Look right, look left, look all around and
then close your eyes and look within, the
mystery's end is within.

Huntington Castle, Clonegal

Look to the Goddess for comfort and guidance, look to the Goddess for safety and truth, look to the Goddess for the way of truth and light, look to the Goddess for the help you require to go on your soul's journey.

The Old Abbey, Huntington Castle, Clonegal

It is for mankind to know that there is plenty for all, abundance for all, fear blocks abundance, fear of lack, fear of shortage, Mother Earth has enough for all, relax, trust and ask as your animals and birds do, as the flowers and trees do, let it be.

The Yew Walk, Huntington Castle, Clonegal

Learn from the ancients, look to the stars, look to the alignment of the stars, the
earth is part of a great alignment, part of a great jigsaw, part of a whole that is
one and that is parts but that is not separate but always whole, always one.
Thank you.

The Wilderness, Huntington Castle, Clonegal

Allow all to run free,
Love only to set free and to be free,
Allow all to be great and true to themselves,
Allow all to speak and say their truth,
Allow all to be as tall as they must be,
As great as they must be from the eyes of God.
Thank you.

Lacey's Distillery, Clonegal

Thank you for your truth,
Thank you for your love,
Thank you for the work,
Thank you for the courage,
Thank you for allowing,
Thank you for the trust
Thank you God.

Giant Redwood at Huntington Castle, Clonegal

It is mighty to see from a higher perspective, to see a bigger picture, look to the bigger picture and look to your role in the bigger picture. Thank you.

St Fiaac's Church,
Clonegal

Halleluaj,
Celebrate,
Glory,
Halleluaj.

River Derry, Clonegal

Allow, allow, allow greatness to flow, stand back and allow your true self to flow, flow as the river does winding its way downhill to the valley below around all obstacles, around resistance, giving way to resistance, going with ease and effortlessness of its openness to the sea where its vastness and power is merged with all other consciousness, as one with another — we are all connected and as one consciousness.

River Slaney near Kildavin

The secret is in the flow of the water, watch how the river charts its course from the hills down into the valley, weaving its way around obstacles, always travelling downhill, this is how life is supposed to be easy and graceful, sometimes fast and furious but in the end, part of a bigger picture as the river enters the sea, the sea the ocean and so on.

Weeping Ash at Adelaide Memorial Church of Christ the Redeemer, Myshall

It is for you and for mankind to love each other, embrace difference, embrace change, grow, develop, move boundaries, cross boundaries, remove limits in action and thought and feeling. Work on yourself, look in the mirror, start with the self, change and improve every day, grow and develop every day — allow greatness and love yourself — there is no need to be afraid — fear not and love every moment of every day. Thank you.

Copper Beech Tree at Adelaide Memorial Church of Christ the Redeemer, Myshall

Allow all to love, allow all to prosper,
Allow all to be as they want to be,
Allow all to dream and to become
What they dream — do not squash
Another's dream, as it is their
Soul quest, their soul life —
Allow, allow, allow. Thank you.

Obar Bhride, Myshall

See the beauty in the stars, in the sky,
See the beauty in the sun, in the moon,
See the beauty in the earth and the Goddess
Of light that shines in all of these.

Yew Trees at Adelaide Memorial Church of Christ the Redeemer, Myshall

Celebrate all that you see growing around you, celebrate all that you eat, all that you drink. Celebrate the abundance of nature, the harvest that is given to you — the abundance of water in your rivers, in your lakes, in your rain. It is for farmers to rejoice in their vocation, rejoice in the privilege of working with Mother Nature. Rejoice in her wisdom, her ancient knowledge of providing for all living things on earth. Thank you.

Augha Church, Nurney

Allow all to be, align yourself with the stars, build your dwellings
according to sacred geometry, there is a method to building that
needs to be adhered to for positive energy, you need to know
where energy lines, energy centres are — build on energy centres
and then it is easier for you to align to your source energy and to
flow with the stream of your own consciousness.

Nurney High Cross

Allow all to be, allow all to prosper in your light, Allow all to be in the greatness of their own light.

River Barrow at Bagenalstown

It is ok to be, and to allow and to just be at one with your surroundings and your space. It is for mankind to know that life flows through us and is in us — that lifeforce is your guide — your light — your lantern — to follow and appreciate and allow. It is for mankind to understand that we are whole and pure as we are if we follow this inner guide and allow and heal.

Killeshin Hills

Halleluaj, glory to the skies, glory to the sun, the moon, the stars,
Awake, awake, awake, open up your eyes to the glory of the power in you to create all that you
see, feel, hear, kneel as before the Lord and give thanks for what is around you — if you
acknowledge and give thanks you will create more beauty in your life as you have shown love
and gratitude, love and gratitude, love and gratitude, thank you.

Old Leighlin Cathedral

Glory be on high, glory, thanks, glory, thanks, gratitude is essential,
always look to what you can give thanks for first before you look to
what you can give out about, look to the light, look to the bright side,
look to the sunshine in the clouds, thank you God for all we have.
Amen.

Beech Trees near Leighlinbridge

Glory be to the creator, majesty to the creator — what an artist, what a magican, what an inventor — glory, glory, glory what can it be? But it just is — Thank you, Thank you, Thank you — allow yourself the stillness and the moment to realise the wow that is all around you, stop, stare, savour and enjoy the glory of it all, thank you God.

Oak Park

Celebrate your love, celebrate your human nature, celebrate the
kindness of the love you share with your friends and family — show it
to your enemy — show it to your opponent — Thank you God.

Haroldstown Dolmen

Allow, allow, allow — it is for you to prosper, to thrive in your environment — but look to your real power, the source of your energy. The source of your energy is not money or power or greed. The source of your energy is the power that runs through you. It is your feelings, your heart, your soul. Tune into this power and all glory and joy are yours always. Thank you.

Eagle Hill, Hacketstown

Allow all to love, allow all to be, allow all to live out their soul's
purpose, allow all to let their heart sing, allow all to be their own
person and their own voice. Thank you.

Clonmore Castle

It is great to love and to be loved, it is great to live with love and by love and for love. Love everyone like they are your own, love everyone like they are your son, love everyone like they are your lover — thank you.

Bulawn Stone, Clonmore

Allow, allow, allow — allow all the beings on your planet to live their
lives in harmony with you. From the mighty oak to the spider to the
mountain to the sea — you are one.

High Cross, Clonmore

Halleluaj Lord God,
Halleluaj Lord God,
Halleluaj Lord God.
Thank you.

The Well, Clonmore

Allow it to shine,
Allow it to be,
Allow it to be all that you are,
You are it, it is you,
It is love.

Old Church, Clonmore

It is good and great to learn, it is a good intention but be sure to know how to learn, learning comes from inside, all that you need to know is inside from the cosmos — thank you — look deep within, make your connection to all that is and you will know all that is.

Standing Stone, near Tullow

Allow yourself all that you are, be all that you are, allow yourself your heart's desire, allow yourself your love, put your love first.

River Duiske, Graiguenamanagh

Allow, allow, allow — it is great to be at one with nature to realise the oneness of consciousness — the oneness of us with one another, with animals, with birds, with insects, with rivers and trees — rejoice and celebrate, rejoice and celebrate, rejoice and celebrate — it is glory, it is peace, it is harmony.

Mount Brandon, Graiguenamanagh

Glory, glory, glory, it is for us all to be, and celebrate
and rejoice in the glory of creation, in the glory of all
that is given, of all that is, of all that is in you and in
mankind and all that is in nature. Allow it to be,
allow it to be and accept that it is and allow all that
is, glory in its difference, glory in its uniqueness,
glory in its individual special uniqueness.

River Barrow at Graiguenamanagh

It is for one and all to love and be loved, that is life's purpose. Love is all that is real, allow and let it flow through your very being in every moment. Live this way and you will always be true to your soul. Thank you God.

Ullard

Glory, glory, glory celebrate all that you see, smell, taste, touch, feel. Celebrate all that is there for you. Now, wake up and know what is there for you now. Feel the love of the consciousness for you and all that has been provided for you, if you could just trust and allow yourself to be.

High Cross
at Ullard

Celebrate and be
thankful, Amen.

Ullard

Allow it all as it is,
Allow it all as you feel it is,
When it feels good, it is good,
When it feels bad, it is bad,
That is your intuition,
That is your pilot,
Do what feels good.
Thank you God.

Beech Trees at a Converted Church, Ullard

Allow, allow, allow, it is for all to know and love themselves and
the lifeforce that flows through them, it is as a mountain stream,
flowing down the mountain, around obstacles, through valleys out
to the sea. Allow life to flow like this, allow life to be like this —
all you want is downstream.

Giant Redwood in Woodstock, Inistioge

It is for you, one and all to listen to your hearts. Listen to the
energy that flows through your heart, express that energy in all
you do big and small and you cannot fail to prosper in
everything you do.

Monkey Puzzle Avenue, Woodstock, Inistioge

It is for you and for your people to go forth and be the people
you were created to be. To be creators of your own destiny, to
allow yourself to be free, to ask questions, follow your heart
and express your joy.

River Nore at Inistioge

Allow, allow yourself to be your whole self, there is much more
to you than your body, imagine the little you, the powerful you
without the limitations of a body, imagine flying free, no time,
no space, no reality as you call it — you are pure positive energy.
You are love, you are life, you are soul and you are spirit.

Well near Tullaherin

It is for you and me to be as one, one in the consciousness
of life, one in the love of the lifeforce, one in the human
brotherhood. Allow yourself to be as one with your
neighbour, allow and let go of right and wrong and
judgement. Only love is right in the end.

Tullaherin Church and Round Tower

It is for mankind to rejoice in the love of each other. Allow
this power to flow and all that you want and ask for will
come into your life. Love yourself first then give that love
to others — blood and strangers alike. Rejoice in this magic
power — called love.

Kings River, Kells

It is good to be free, it is good to make your own decisions, it is
good to step into the power God has given and love the power
that flows through you from God. The power that is in all
living things and connects you to all living things.

Kells Priory

It is for mankind to love one another and all living beings, all animals, plants, insects, birds, trees. Love one another, work in love, labour in love, the love is the true word of God.

Yew Tree in old graveyard, Kells Priory

Mankind will flourish when they allow themselves and others to live in harmony and inner peace, allow themselves to release and trust in the lifeforce that flows through all living things, allowing the lifeforce to provide for them and to give them nourishment and food for life's journey.

It is for mankind to speak and act in love, love is the positive energy that lives on forever. Love is the eternal juice and flow that is life and after life. Say it, do it, breathe it. Love is the only life and path that people need and then fear will go. Love will always shine through fear. Love will always shine through darkness.

High Cross at Kilree Round Tower

It is for us as humans to evolve spiritually from lifetime to lifetime — to ask the big questions and receive answers from the Lord — talk directly to the Lord — communicate with the Lord flowing through you — through silent retreat and meditation and work for the Lord with love and kindness always. Halleluaj, Christ is King. Halleluaj, Christ is King.

Beech Tree, Kilree Round Tower

It is for you to understand that I am you and you
are me — we are one for all is connected all is
linked, all is one. You are a tree, I am a person
this is just the way it is, now and always till the
end of time. Thank you God.

St. Brigid's Well, near Kilree Round Tower

Halleluaj Christ is King, follow the energy, allow, allow, allow, it
is for you to follow the calling, follow the messages, follow your
instincts, follow your gut — your soul knows what it is doing,
always for your highest good — trust and allow.

River Nore at Thomastown

Allow all to be as you wish you could be in your deepest soul — what you see as faults within others, need to be addressed within yourself — allow yourself to look at your inner being and allow yourself to improve, progress, you deserve it — you want it — ask and you will receive the guidance you need.

Waterfall at Kilfane Glen

Allow yourself freedom to express your inner knowing, your inner wisdom, you
know more than you have learnt this lifetime, tap into all your resources and
allow your eternity to shine, allow your wisdom to lead you, this is what is
really meant by learning the lessons of history — you have been here before
and learnt many lessons, your soul knows this — learn to acknowledge this and
tap into that resource — it is the greatest untapped resource known to man.

Thomastown Church

Halleluaj, praise for the sunshine, praise for the rain, praise for the wind, praise for the sky, praise for the moon, praise the stars, praise the universe, praise the galaxy of dreams of mankind.

Killminich, near Thomastown

Halleluaj you are blessed to be in this land of saints and scholars. Read, learn and absorb their energy — yours is the legacy of their learning, their progress through time, yours is the gift of education, the gift of reading, writing, art and science — celebrate, appreciate and rejoice.

Jerpoint Abbey

Halleluaj, Christ is King. Halleluaj it is for you to know that the glory of God is served through love. Love is the answer to all life's big questions — allow love to flow through your veins, your being, your very core. Halleluaj, Christ is King. Thank you God.

Beech Trees near Tullagher

Celebrate, breathe the air, drink in nature, let the
greenness heal you, let the Green Man energy heal
you, spend time in nature, it is part of you, you are
part of it — let it be your mainstay, let it be your
friend — treat it as you would your family, love it
as you would your family — live with it as you
would with the ones you love most.

Three Friars near Tullagher

Allow, allow, allow, love is freedom, love is peace, love is harmony, love is in your heart not your mind. Sink into your hearts, your minds are for thinking only, your heart is more powerful, these are your feelings — follow your heart — not your mind — life is for loving not for thinking that thoughts are superior — love conquers all.

Discovery Park, Castlecomer

It is for mankind to know working with nature is the key to all
bounty, all true abundance and inner peace and harmony, all that
exploit Mother Nature will never have eternal peace or inner peace
— over and over till the lesson is learnt, turmoil will prevail.

South Cross at St James Church, Castledermot

Halleluaj Christ King — allow people to live their own lives, let
them be, love them for who they are not what they are, in the name
of grace and humanity — allow all to be part of your consciousness
as you are part of theirs.

Oak Tree at St James Church, Castledermot

It is for all of us to be — go inside yourself, deep in the well of peace and
tranquility quieten your mind, allow your soul to speak, listen to the soul,
listen to your own wisdom.

Sycamore Tree at St James Church,
Castledermot

Infinite intelligence is there for everyone — leap in
faith, ask in faith, trust in the lifeforce, trust in
yourself and then allow.

North Cross at St James Church, Castledermot

In the name of the glory of God allow yourself to be all that you can be, all that you want to be, allow all that you dream you can be — it is yours, ask and it is given to the glory of the lifeforce that flows through you and all living things.

Yew Tree at St James Church, Castledermot

Nature is a retreat for all, open your eyes — open your senses, open your heart to its power, so many people are closed and ignorant to this power, they wonder why life is hard and yet they do not love and respect this power, this lifeforce that is there for their love and joy. Instead they abuse and take and take — give and give and you will receive the power, the lifeforce of the light, the love, the power behind life itself. Allow nature to teach and love you.

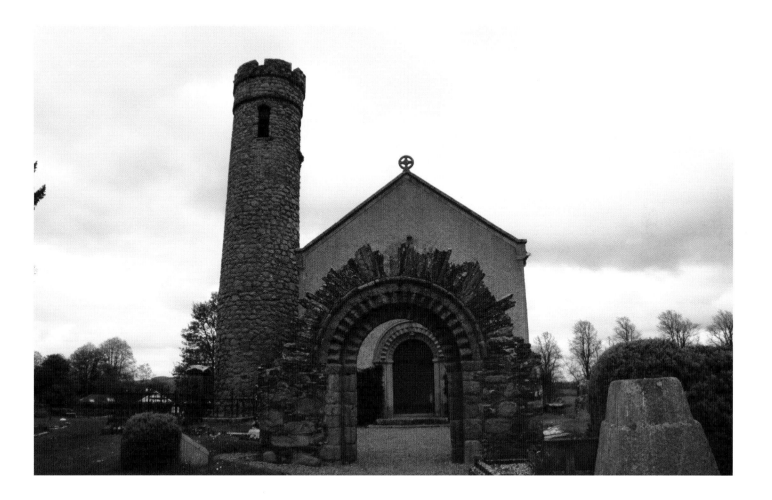

South Hog-back at St James Church, Castledermot

Halleluaj to Christ, Halleluaj to Christ, celebrate life, love life, live life in joy — allow the positive energy only to flow — allow, allow, allow the beauty of your soul to run through your veins — the negative energy is outshone by the light — allow the love and beauty of your consciousness, your soul, your spirit to shine.

These are the only examples in Ireland of Hog-backs, a scandavian-type grave marker

North Hog-back St James Church, Castledermot

Glory be to God — your lifeforce is beautiful, your lifeforce is love,
your lifeforce is life — it is there for you always — open up your third
eye — open up your heart to the lifeforce on your planet, in your
universe, in your life.

The Friary, Castledermot

It is for all mankind to realise that they need to wake up, focus on the
positive, focus on the good, focus on the creativity — focus on the
love — focus on the light — the more you focus the more you get, so
all this focus on negative and dark energy just brings more of it.
Wake up — live in love and light.

Lime Trees at St James Church, Castledermot

It is wonderful to be in nature, it is wonderful to see nature to really see nature, to see all that is in nature. Take your time — immerse yourself in the joy and love of nature and all its consciousness and all its spirit.

Grand canal, Naas

Celebrate flight, celebrate your heritage in a constructive way, ask why did we create that, do not look to blame others, look within, the lessons of history are within, your past as a nation was created to learn soul lessons, to know the meaning look in the mirror and ask what am I to learn.

Moone High Cross

Allow all to be themselves,
Allow all to love themselves,
Allow all to love the people they want,
Allow all to believe in love,
Allow all to live in love.

The Holed High Cross at Moone

*Halleluaj celebrate love, live in love, worship God in love,
allow love, allow love in all things — you will reap the
rewards of heaven in your life everyday if all you do, say,
think, believe, feel is love.*

Knockaulin, Kilcullen
(Dún Ailinne — Royal Site of Leinster)

Allow love and freedom in your being. Then the
Universe feels that vibration and responds to that
want that you are expessing vibrationally and gives it
to you. So it is the feeling you give virationally that
the Universe responds to. Thank you God.

Old Kilcullen Round Tower and High Crosses

It is for mankind to celebrate the goodness and abundance around them, the fruitful hedgerows, the fertile land, the many meats, the clean rivers and streams. It is a bounty of care from Mother Earth and the gods of greenery. Give thanks and be full.

Standing Stone, Near Kilcullen

Look to the stars, the cosmos, for your place in the
greater scheme of things, sacred geometry and
astrology are the sciences to study to know the jigsaw
piece that you are in the wonder of the universe.

Hills around Coolkenno

Allow all to be, all to be as they are, allow to be just the
way they are, divine beings of the creator, perfect in this
moment as beings of love and light, beings of energy,
beings of vibration, they are as they are and all is well.
Thank you.

Hills around Kilquiggan

Allow yourself to see wonder, to see the miracle of life,
affirm it daily, give thanks for it daily, it is a miracle daily
to be and to be loved, to love and to be loved, to be a part
of one, to be a part of all, to be a part of all that is and
always will be. Thank you God.

Grove of trees, Aghowle

Celebrate your maker, celebrate the one who loves all aspects of you great and good, poor and pure, rich and full. It is for you to know every thought, every moment, every belief, every feeling, every emotion, every action. Allow yourself to know that what feels good, is good — what feels like fear, is fear.

Aghowle Hills

Celebrate like there is no tomorrow, dance like this is the only moment, let go, let go, let go, feel who you truly are, not what you work at, not who you are married to or a child of, who are you? Do you know who you are yourself? Wake up, the time is now, let it be, love it, live it now. Thank you.

Aghowle Church

Allow mankind to be, allow each other to be on a personal level, allow all to love and be loved. Allow all to be as one and to be themselves as they see themselves. Love them no matter what they do or say — look beyond the action to the being and the true potential of the being.

Yew Tree at Aghowle Church

Celebrate your truth,
Celebrate your true nature,
Celebrate your true vision,
Your true voice — let it
speak and know
that it is good and true.

High Cross, Aghowle Church

Celebrate the Lord,
Celebrate the Lord,
See that it is good.

Grove of trees, Aghowle Church

Celebrate your connection to each other. Your connection to one another in all that you are and you be, celebrate the connection that gives all things life — that is love.

Lime Trees, Munny Lodge

Allow yourself be what you want to be, parents
let go of your children, they are not yours to hold
back, they are creators in their own right, love
and protect them but allow them to be all that
they want to be for better or worse, it is their
path. Thank you.

Baltinglass Hills

Love yourself, love mankind, love your
animals and the wild animals, love the
birds and the bees, love the mountains and
the stream, fill your heart and pour it out
every day, it is a never ending flow of light,
it is eternity and pure love, unconditional
love, acceptance and light. Let it flow.
Thank you.

Baltinglass Abbey

Allow, allow, allow, it is much more than tolerance, let go of all
resistance and allow yourself and others to just be in their souls,
in their hearts, as they are, as they are divine and perfect as they
are — let go of thought and judgement and see from your heart
with love and acceptance.

Castleruddery Embanked Stone Circle

Let all be, let yourself be, all is well, work with nature, work within yourself and expand your vibration, expand your horizons, expand the consciousness that is you, and that which connects you to all living beings — expand and know that you are all and all is you, you are one and one is you.

St Patrick's, Kiltegan

Glory, glory, glory, praise to the God of nature, see the natural wonder that you are and celebrate yourself, love yourself so you can love God. Thank you.

Ballinabarry Gap

Allow yourself magic, allow yourself miracles, allow yourself
the essence of life, the glory of life, look for answers within
yourself — heal yourself — all is well — thank you.

Donoughmone near Donard

Allow greatness — follow your dreams, live in your heart
— think big, thoughts become things — think good, happy,
joyous thoughts — thank you God.

Church Mountain

Allow all to be commanding in what they want, what
they are here to create, what they are here to do, what
their soul's journey is — if you put another down,
you put yourself down, if you keep another down,
you keep yourself down.

West Wicklow Mountains

It is splendid what you see, what you hear, what you feel — allow yourself to fully see, hear and feel — allow yourself to be and to be all that you can be — listen to the voice within — no other voice is valid to you and your life's work and fun.

Glen of Imaal

Celebrate all that is seen and
unseen, celebrate the power
behind the seen, celebrate
the lifegiver, celebrate the
lifeforce, the breath of life
that is and is not and is the
only source of life.

River Slaney at Seskin Bridge, Glen of Imail

Allow the flow, allow the movement, always moving, never permanent, only ever impermanence — flow, flow, flow — all you want, all you need is downstream.

Keadeen Mountain

Glory and praise to the maker, look for the maker in you, look
for how to express creativity that is you and you are it. It is for
you to create your own life, live life by creating what you want
not letting life happen by default — you are the life artist —
enjoy your creation — Thank you God.

Lugnaquilla Mountain

Glory, glory, Halleluaj, it is a fine thing to reach into the sky beyond
the clouds and to see all around in this beautiful landscape, it is easy
to marvel at God from up here. Thank you God.

Tree Fungus, Glen of Imail

Lifegiver is in you, light is in you to shine, shine your light, sing
your song, cry from the heart, speak your truth — thank you God.

Aghavannagh

Allow yourself glory, allow yourself love, pleasure in a pure loving
manner that allows all to prosper, all to thrive, that is not selfish or
cruel, or ignorant or prejudiced, allow your enemy your love,
forgive your enemy, forgive yourself.

Hawthorn Tree on Stony Earth Bank, Aghavannagh

It is for mankind to know that they are a part of the cosmos,
the heavens, they are divine beings, they are part of the
consciousness, as are the animals, the birds and the trees.
They are no more no less than the birds and the bees, no
more no less that the animals and the plants — it is to be a
part of this, in harmony with this that is the human
endeavour, the challenge for the vision of mankind.

Woods on the Rathdrum to Laragh Road

Celebrate the feeling of joy in your heart — feel the joy in your fingertips and in your toes, it is the joy of living in the moment, the joy of realising that the only time is now, the only time is present in this moment and all is well.

Near Rathdangan

Celebrate the green,
celebrate the leaves,
celebrate the insects,
the birds, the rodents,
the butterflies, the
branches, the moss,
the life that makes up
this place, this home
of many species,
living in harmony.

Mount Usher Gardens

Celebrate your surroundings, the colour, the
smells, the true sense of your being that is all
around you in every living thing that you touch,
see, feel and know is your sense of being, of life,
of love, of glory — thank you.

River Avondale

Allow yourself all that you are, all that you can be, no boundaries
set by other people need affect you — no limits of this man —
influenced world can impinge on your divine trust — allow
yourself to speak and live your truth every moment of every day.

Clara Vale

Allow yourself to be immersed in the beauty and healing of greenness.
Greenness soothes the soul, brings inner peace and contentment — and
allows you to be at one with yourself and connect your consciousness to
nature and all its bounty — allow yourself to feel the connection with
nature and give thanks for its bounty and your participation in it.

Ballygannon Woods near Laragh

Nature is a resource to be used by mankind for their good, for their everyday necessary living and for their appreciation and leisure. It is not meant for human abuse and for means of accumulation and greed. The squirrel hoards to carry it over winter, the human hoards out of fear, fear of lack, there is no lack on earth, there is only abundance from the creator. It is fear and only fear that causes lack, and only love of fellow mankind and fellow consciousness that brings the abundance into sight.

Thank you.

Meeting of the Waters, Avoca

It is for mankind to look to the wisdom of the stars, look to sacred geometry, to fully understand the energy, the vibration of your planet. The earth is aligned with other stars in the universe, with other planetary energy lines. See that the earth is a part of this greater universe, look at your world, your life in this context and all will seem clearer. Thank you.

Round Tower, Glendalough

Glory, glory, glory —
let all live in peace
and harmony working
with God's bounty to
enlighten mankind, to
educate and be with
the one that is us all
and is in us all —
running through us
like a power, like a
mighty river current,
like a tidal wave of
Christ, like you, know
your source.

St. Kevin's Kitchen, Glendalough

Halleluaj all is in being, all is in knowing how to be, knowing the silence, knowing the stillness, knowing the Lord in the stillness of the soul, in the quietness of the mind, in the peace of the spirit.

High Cross, Glendalough

Celebrate all, celebrate love, celebrate life in love and love all — thank you.

Forest Path from Glendalough to Laragh

Nature is your friend but nature is a powerful friend, do not cross a powerful friend, trust and love depend on being faithful and working with your friend. Allow your love of your friend to be in all your thoughts and actions towards that friend always.

St. Saviour's Church, Glendalough

Celebrate love, celebrate friendship, celebrate fellowship,
love underpins a happy life, love underpins a successful life
— love, love, love always, in your heart not your head.

Glendasan River, Glendalough

Celebrate, oh celebrate all is love and light, all is for each other and is for you and your life to live and share, live and love, live and be, live and be free, live for yourself but live for each other. Do not lose the connection to your lifeforce or else the light dims and life becomes a struggle rather than the joy of creation that it truly is and can be everyday every way always.

Lower Lake, Glendalough

It is for mankind to know that all that is required is to love each other, block the darkness by letting in the light, the light is love, the light is the greatest power in all the world — harness the light, harness the love to conquer all darkness, all feeling bad, all feeling low, all feeling depressed, let the light in and all mankind can feel is love, joy, happiness and love.

Upper Lake, Glendalough

Allow and wish and ask for all you want — know what you want — reflect, be silent and discover your own heart, listen to your heart, follow your heart, even when the way does not seem like it is correct or right, tune into your heart, your heart is the gateway to your soul, to know your soul tune in and listen to your heart. Thank you.

The Reefert Church, Glendalough

Glory to God, glory to Christ, all is well, all is aligned to the stars
and the cosmos, all is vibrationally aligned to source energy, know
that this is the divine state, this is the holy way of life, to live in
the divine flow of your energy with the Lord's energy.

Caher, Glendalough

Allow the glory of all your being to shine in your
natural greatness that is in each and every being on
earth, human, mammal, bird, tree, plant, fish, reptile,
you know this — allow this.

St. Kevin's Cell, Glendalough

Allow yourself your own love of self, your own love of
spirit, your own love of body, your own love of soul,
your own love of all that is you and makes up you, that
makes you the unique individual being that you are.
Thank you.

Ruin at Glendalough

It is for you to know in your heart that all is well,
all is perfect in the moment, all is as it needs to be
at this time. All is as it is the way you see it but all
is also an illusion of time and space that is eternity.
Look at all from different levels of perception and
wisdom will follow. Thank you.

Poulanass Waterfall, Glendalough

Glory be, glory to the alignment of stars, the alignment of cosmos, the alignment of the universe that has created this precious centre of energy, this precious centre of communication with the divine realms. This precious centre of education from the divine to humans on earth. The connection is still there for people who seek it out — the heavens are always looking to communicate with people who ask — ask and it is given — ask and answers will follow in your life — love of life, love of self, love of fellow beings, love of Mother Earth — allow and look for the knowledge within — look for the Lord, the divine that flows through you and is you. Thank you.

Munny Lower

Allow splendour and allow splendour of love and splendour of joy
— allow expression of feeling — welcome expression of feeling
and welcome their guidance for a happy life.

Stoneyfort River

It is for mankind to allow themselves to express their true love and feelings for all that they wish to know. It is for mankind to allow one another to love and to be loved and to allow freedom to express all that is within their body and soul. Allow others to be and allow yourself to be always and all will be well and connected to source energy, white light, eternal love.

Sycamore Tree at Leopardstown Business Park

It is to allow the love, the lifeforce to work through you, to flow without resistance through you — that is the challenge of every individual — to stop blocking and resisting the divine flow of love, the current of life, the instrument of energy, the white light, that is what is required by an individual to experience pure joy and satisfaction in life and to truly be at one with themselves and with all beings on this earth.

Sycamore Tree at Roundabout, Leopardstown Business Park

It is for you and me and our fellow man to join as one and to understand that all is love, all is one — we are all connected by the same energy, the same lifeforce — we are all vibration, we all have thoughts, feelings and physical bodies but it is our spirits that are connected and are as one. See others as spirits residing in physical vessels — look to their core for the connection and you will see that we are all the same, all one.

Beech Trees, Leopardstown Business Park

Allow yourself to relax and still your mind — quieten the chatter, the internal strife, the external criticism, self doubt, questioning — quieten it all as you would if the most beautiful creature you ever saw stood before you, quieten as you would if you wanted to reach out and touch that creature without frightening it away, gently, quietly, slowly, gently, quietly, slowly — this is how you should shut down the mind so that you can go deeper into yourself and the wisdom that lies deep in every human being.

North High Cross at Clonmacnoise

Halleluaj, allow mankind to be themselves, in order to prosper ask
God's help — the God that flows through you — tap into your own
power — follow your own guidance system — follow your own heart.

South High Cross at Clonmacnoise

Rejoice in love, rejoice in life, allow the good in, do not give attention to the bad, that only brings more of it — look to the good only and you will only have good in your life.

The Abbey at Clonmacnoise

Halleluaj live in communion with nature — respect and love nature — allow the natural world to be your guide and helper — connect to that power — rejoice in that power and prosper in that power.

River Shannon at Clonmacnoise

Allow all your friends to be your enemies and all
your enemies to be your friends — love
everyone, not just a few, love with all your heart
with no conditions, no demands, no expectations
— allow your friends and enemies to be as one,
mankind is your brother, your sister, your
mother, your father and your child.

Ruin of Clonmacnoise Castle

Allow yourself to be as great as God created you to be
— stop blocking and shying away from greatness —
each human being has greatness in them if they
believe and allow.

Round Tower, Killala

Halleluaj celebrate the view,
celebrate the power of the
sea, celebrate the seabirds,
celebrate the breaking waves,
celebrate the sand dunes,
celebrate life's abundance,
celebrate all the goodness in
front of your eyes and around
your energy,
celebrate all the Lord has
given you — thank you.

Killala Bay

Halleluaj celebrate your life's gifts, life's providence, life's love, life's friends, celebrate the wonder of life, the wonder of life — see the wonder of life all else is an illusion, a lesson for the soul allow it to pass and ask to know the lesson.

Palmerstown River near Killala

It is for mankind to know that all is well, all is as it should be, allow and relax, see from a larger higher perspective, do not allow day to day matters to distract your focus from what is really important, on what is really real in life, on what truly matters — love of self, mankind and your planet, universe — your world — what you are and what everything is — the lifeforce of love. Love is all that matters.

Down Patrick Head

Halleluaj glory be to the lifeforce, celebrate the wild pure force of nature, celebrate the power of nature, celebrate the beauty of nature, the awesome splendour of nature — glory, glory, glory.

Céide Fields

It is for us to realise that the nature and earth we have been given is enough to live from without exploitation, without scarring, without wounding, all is well, there is abundance, when Mother Earth is worked with and respected, She will flourish and continue to produce and produce. When She is raped of natural resources, natural law is violated — the abundance ends.

Rosserk Friary

Allow, allow, allow, allow all the people to be as one, allow
all people to love, allow people to be and to live as is for
them, allow people to feel good in their own way, allow
people to live, love and work in their own way.

Earth Mound beside Rosserk Friary

Celebrate life's mystery, you don't need to know all, you do not always need explanation, accept the mystery of life in all its glory. It is a positive thing to follow your feelings and go with what feels good and what feels best for you. It is for you to allow your life to flow in this manner and celebrate life in its true glory.

River Moy, Ballina

Celebrate all that you see and give thanks. All is well in this moment as you are going with your flow. Thank you for your patience, thank you for your love. See now with an open mind how good life can feel. Thank you God.

Easkey River

Give praise to the energy that creates all, give praise to the lifeforce, the creator, give praise to the force that has shaped our world — wake up and truly see — allow yourself to see the glory, the splendour, the beauty of the creator and all that the divine energy has created.

Ben Bulben

Praise, glory, halleluaj, look at your life, look at your abundance, give thanks without hesitation, without resistance, without resentment. Look to your abundance, look to the quality of your life — who is making the decision? Who is creating your reality? Step into your own power, use your mind, spirit and soul to create the life experience you want and give thanks for the glory of this gift.

Split Rock at Cashey

Give praise to the power of the creator who created such
abundance for mankind to live in harmony and peace. Give
praise for all the abundance that allows mankind happiness
and joy if they could just see from the divine that is in them
they would see this and always be happy and joyful.

Knocknarea

Celebrate, celebrate, celebrate nature in all its splendour, all its glory, all
its magnificence. Celebrate the air you breathe, the sky above you, the
grass beneath you, celebrate the plants that grow, the animals that want to
live in harmony and peace with you. Celebrate all the living beings around
you, celebrate all mankind around. Celebrate and live in joyful love.

Ballygawley Mountains

Celebrate the air you breathe, the natural world around you, the way your spirit soars when in nature, that is Green Man energy, love and respect the energy of nature, your natural environment, the provider of all food, water and natural resources, love, respect and honour and your life will always be filled with love, joy and abundance.

Temple House Lake, Ballymote

Thank you for your
sweetness,
Thank you for
your love,
Thank you for the
gathering of mind,
body and spirit,
Go and soar now
in the world,
Thank you.

Glory be to the Goddess, it is for all to recognise the power of the feminine, it is for all to be at one with nature and to recognise Mother Earth. It is for all to live and work in harmony with Mother Nature and her power — allow nature to be your provider, your joy, your lifeforce — allow yourself to be immersed and connected to the lifeforce of nature, the power of the Green Man, the power of Mother Nature and reap the harvest and give thanks.

Carrowmore Megalithic Cemetery

Align with the stars, the earth is but a small part of the universal
system of planets — look to the skies and align your hearts,
minds and souls with the kingdoms in the sky.

Atlantic Ocean, off Sligo Coast

Your own spirit is as great as the ocean, as powerful, as pure, wake up and see that you are powerful and beautiful and strong, use for good, use for your fellow mankind and all that live with you on your planet earth.

The Burren

Poulnabrone, The Burren

It is for mankind to understand that time is timeless, time is fast, a measurement in eternity, one lifetime is but a blink in the grand scheme of things — timelessness is beyond human comprehension but until humans grasp it they will always be limited by their lack of comprehension of God and the power of the universe.

Caherconnell Stone Fort, The Burren

It is for mankind to be aware that the earth is for the glory of the lifeforce, it is expressed in every blade of grass, every buzzing of the bees, every flutter of a butterfly's wing, allow yourself to feel and enjoy the splendour allow it to pulsate in your every being — that is the secret of life — just that — that is all.

Gleninsheen Wedge Tomb, The Burren

It is for mankind to understand the wonders of nature and the splendour of the earth they live on — it has been created by the lifeforce to show mankind the glory of the lifeforce but mankind loses focus and focuses on trivial matters like material wealth and all the time the glory is in them but they are disconnected from it. Wake up and feel the lifeforce, the glory within. Halleluaj.

Kilfeorna Crosses, Kilfeorna

It is with joy we give thanks for all creation and for mankind and the experience of life in the Lord's kingdom.
It is for the glory of God we celebrate the coming of the Kingdom of God to serve the people of the earth.
Thank you God. Halleluaj, thank you God.

The North Cross, Kilfeorna

Halleluaj it is with joy that we celebrate the life giver, the spirit that is in us all thanks to you for our lifeforce, the gift to all creation, the heartbeat of every living thing. Halleluaj.

The "Doorty" Cross, Kilfeorna

Halleluaj, it is for us to give thanks and be fulfilled with the joy of the Lord our God for the glory of our being and the joy and light and love that is life and is what we are here to experience. Halleluaj.